Communications Machines

Library of Congress Number: 79-27718

1 2 3 4 5 6 7 8 9 0 84 83 82 81 80

Printed in the United States of America.

Library of Congress Cataloging in Publication Data

Howard, Sam.
    Communications machines.

    Includes index.
    SUMMARY: Discusses the different machines and sys-
tems that help relay information across this country,
across the oceans, and through space.
    1. Telecommunication—Juvenile literature.
[1. Telecommunication. 2. Communication] I. Title.
TK5102.4.H68   621.38   79-27718
ISBN 0-8172-1335-X lib. bdg.

Photographs appear through the courtesy of the following:
American Telephone & Telegraph: pp. 8-13
David Janzer: pp. 3, 20, 21
Gene Dodd: p. 4
Hughes: cover, pp. 28-30
Morley Johnson: pp. 5-7, 14-19
Storer Broadcasting/Morley Johnson: pp. 22-27

communications
MACHINES

Sam Howard

RAINTREE CHILDRENS BOOKS
Milwaukee • Toronto • Melbourne • London

The traffic light turns green. The bus starts down the street. A light beams from a lighthouse. The boat steers away. What do these things have in common? They are signals and they give people information. When the traffic light is green, the bus driver knows it is safe to go.

When the sailor can see the lighthouse, the boat is coming too close to shore. Signals like these are simple kinds of communication. Communication is sharing ideas and information. This book is about some machines used in various kinds of communication.

This man is a bridge tender. He is needed to work these controls. He communicates messages using the instruments on this panel. He lets people know when the bridge will go up to let a boat pass. First he turns on one switch, and red lights begin to flash. Then he turns a switch to start bells clanging.

These signals warn people to stop. The bridge tender is in this little building with the bell. He turns another lever to lower the bridge gates on the street. Cars will stop. This man will also turn lights on for the people on the boat to see. These lights help them navigate. The bridge tender gives this information by using lights and noise.

Telephones are used everyday by almost everybody. People can talk to each other from one house to another or from one country to another. How does a telephone work? The mouthpiece is a transmitter. It picks up sound waves made by your voice. These sound waves are changed into electrical waves. They are then carried to another phone. The earpiece on that phone is a receiver.

Here the electrical waves will change back into sound waves—your voice. But placing a call takes more than just a transmitter and receiver. There is an electronic system involved. Cables and wires are a part of this system. Below, a man is installing underground telephone cables. These cables from homes meet at a terminal box.

The cables lead from the terminal box to a central office. There are over 150 million phones in the United States. Each one is connected to special equipment at a central office. The special equipment looks like this. Let's say you want to call this number: 555-4567. The first three numbers

ocate the central office you need.
he last four numbers identify the
articular phone connected to that
entral office.

The telephone company uses
nany computers to help with its
ob. Some computers can tell people
f the telephone equipment is
vorking properly.

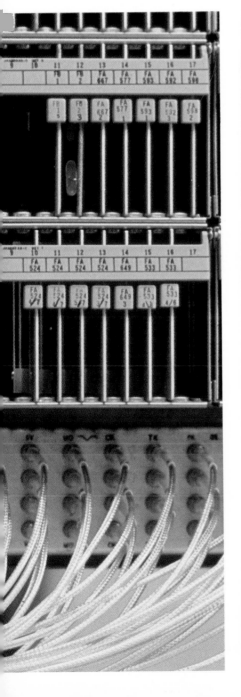

If it is not, other computers will help locate the problem. These men are using one to do just that. Once the problem is found the dispatcher can send someone to fix the telephone equipment. The dispatcher is using the map.

This operator is using a computer to help a customer. She is trying to locate a phone number.

Telephones make it possible to communicate with people almost anywhere. Across the street. In another state. Around the world. A telephone company has many ways to send your voice. One way is through a microwave tower like this. Your voice is carried through the air on radio waves. That's how you can talk with someone on a ship or an airplane.

The huge rolls of paper below are feeding into a printing press that will print a newspaper. The next few pages will show you how a modern newspaper gets all the words and pictures into print. Many newspapers have modern machines that make that job fast.

The news story is the heart of a newspaper. First, a reporter gets a story to a newspaper office.

The woman below is entering the story, or copy, into a VDT. A VDT is like a typewriter, but the words come onto a television screen instead of paper. The VDT is connected to a computer that keeps all the day's copy in its memory. The men in the small pictures are putting advertisements into VDTs.

A news editor gets the copy back on another VDT screen to make changes. When the copy is final, a button is pushed, and the copy is automatically set in lines of type. The lines of type come out of the typesetting machine on paper.

The copy and pictures then go to the makeup room. Here they are pasted-up the way they will look on the printed page. Next, the pasted-up pages go to the engraving room. The pages are photographed with special large cameras.

The films of the pages then go to a platemaking machine. A very bright light goes through the film, and the image is transferred to a thin metal plate. From that, the final printing plate is made.

The printing plate fits around large cylinders on the printing press. Finally, all the day's news and advertisements are ready to be printed.

The press starts rolling. The huge paper rolls feed into the press. And out come printed newspapers.

Radios are seen and heard everywhere. You can hear the news or listen to a favorite song. Ever wonder how one works? The disc jockey, or DJ works in a sound room like this. Sometimes the DJ talks into a microphone. Other times music is played into one. The microphone changes the sound waves into an electric current. The current goes through a wire. The wire leads to a transmitter.

Below is a transmitter. It will amplify, or strengthen, the current. Then the current travels to an antenna. The antenna causes the current to change into radio waves. The radio waves are sent out from the antenna. Some of them will find your radio's antenna. Inside your radio, these waves change back into electric ones. Then these change into sound waves. And that's how you hear talk and music.

You have seen several ways people use machines to communicate. Still another, but more complicated way, is television Television is probably the most popular form of communication. People around the world spend hours watching it every day.

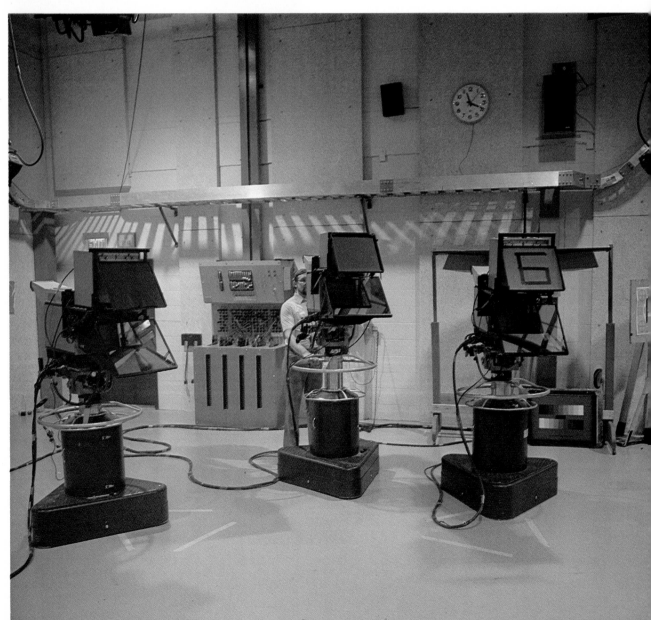

This is a television studio. The news reporter is getting ready to go on air." He gets some of the news from a wire service machine like the one on the right. A special TV camera takes moving pictures of this man. Inside this camera electronic images are formed.

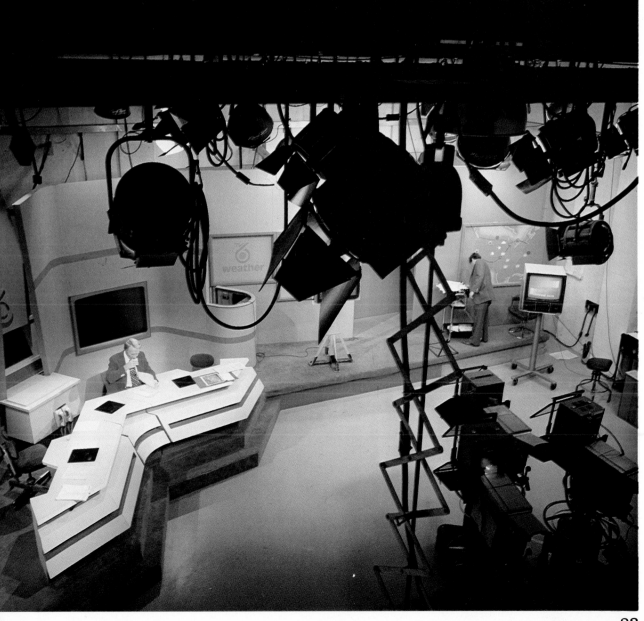

Electric current is made from these images. This current then goes to transmitter. So do the sounds picked up by the microphone. The current then goes to an antenna. The antenna changes the current into TV and radio waves. These reach your TV antenna and finally your TV set.

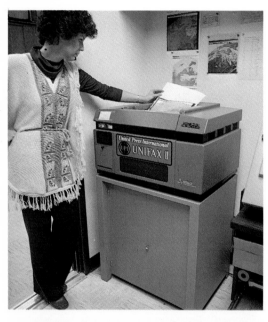

Many communications machines are used at a TV station. On the left-hand page are machines that give weather information. International weather news comes from the Unifax II. Weather radar is produced by the machine below it. On this page is some modern electronic news gathering equipment.

This is the master control room of a television station. These technicians have final control of the picture and sound before it goes on the air. They make sure the picture and sound are the best they can be before they reach your TV set.

TV stations can receive news
relayed by a satellite. But they must
have a receiver. This dish is a
receiver. It gets signals from a
satellite thousands of miles in
space. TV stations and other
businesses in communications rent
satellites as they need them.

The most important
development in communications is
the communications satellite. It can
relay information all over the world
in seconds. It must be launched in
orbit in space. Solar cells provide
the energy it needs.

A satellite receives signals from
earth. It amplifies these signals and
sends them back. On the left is a
weather satellite called the GMS 1.
Below to the left is the Westar. To
the right is the Marisat. They relay
voices and other data.

The satellite on the left is the Anik. It relays TV and phone signals to 110 stations in Canada. Below is the Comstar. It can relay over 18,000 phone calls at once.

Life is always changing. From signal to satellite, machines keep us informed of these changes.

GLOSSARY

antenna	The part of a communications machine or system that sends and receives waves.
communication	The process of exchanging information between people.
communications satellite	A communications machine that is launched into orbit. A satellite receives communication signals and relays them to another place.
instrument panel	A panel, or board, where controls and dials are located.
lighthouse	A tower that has a strong light, which is a signal for ships.
memory	The part of a computer that can store information for later use.
microphone	A communications machine that changes sounds into electric current.
microwave tower	A tower that sends microwaves (such as those from a telephone transmitter) through the air.
platemaking machine	A machine that makes printing plates from film.
printing press	A machine that prints newspapers, books, magazines, and other printed matter.
receiver	The part of a telephone that lets the user hear the voice from the person on the other end.
signal	Something—such as a sound or a color—that gives a warning or other information.
solar cell	A battery that gets power from the sun.
transmitter	The part of a telephone that changes sound to electric current so that the sound can be sent to the other end.
typesetting machine	A machine that sets copy in lines of type.

INDEX